Frayed Linens

Frayed Linens

Marilyn Bowering

singular fiction, poetry, nonfiction, translation, drama, and graphic books

Library and Archives Canada Cataloguing in Publication

Title: Frayed linens / Marilyn Bowering.
Names: Bowering, Marilyn, author.
Description: Includes bibliographical references.
Identifiers: Canadiana (print) 20250292157 | Canadiana (ebook) 20250292203 | ISBN 9781990773679 (softcover) | ISBN 9781990773686 (EPUB) | ISBN 9781990773709 (PDF) | ISBN 9781990773693 (Kindle)
Subjects: LCGFT: Poetry.
Classification: LCC PS8553.O9 F73 2025 | DDC C811/.54—dc23

Book and cover designed by Maria Eydmans
Cover and interior photographs © Xan Shian
Typeset in Bembo, Granjon, Zapfinio, and Birka fonts at Moons of Jupiter Studios

Published by Exile Editions Ltd ~ www.ExileEditions.com
144483 Southgate Road 14, Holstein, Ontario, N0G 2A0

Printed and bound in Canada by Gauvin

We gratefully acknowledge the Government of Canada and Ontario Creates for their financial support toward our publishing activities.

Canadian sales representation:
The Canadian Manda Group, 664 Annette Street,
Toronto ON M6S 2C8 www.mandagroup.com 416 516 0911

North American and international distribution, and U.S. sales:
Independent Publishers Group, 814 North Franklin Street,
Chicago IL 60610 www.ipgbook.com toll free: 1 800 888 4741

for Michael and the little Family

God before me, God behind me,
God over me, God below me,
I on Thy path, O God,
Which shall never be darkened.
Augury of Mary

This Was Dark

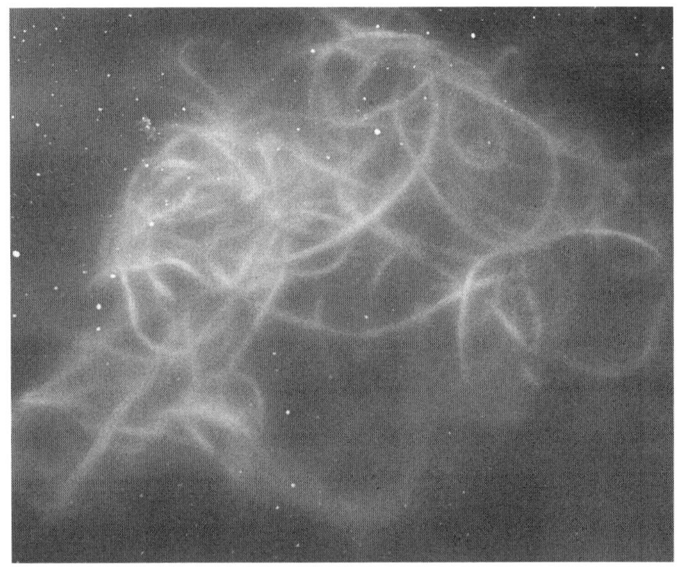

Horror / This Is What Happened

Some day you will be one of those who lived long ago.

—Pär Lagerkvist

"The horror came on hoof and bone with shattered shoes
and a pail of ashes," my mother said to me.

"It must be murdered, rolled downstairs and buried in the back
until its flesh slips and its skeleton sings."

Someone shuffled in the kitchen, made soup,
and rattled loaf tins. Someone scraped the roof with torn fingernails.

It was the end of a species, a whale that no one remembered,
all diaphanous soul, its eyes like jellyfish

squeezing water into the ocean.
"You, dead things, get up," my mother said. I lay quiet.

"It is dark enough now to pinch wings from your
natural body's back," she said.

A dog hulked beneath a broken chair in the shed:
it howled until everything alive ran into the graveyard

of homeless words.

I got up to salvage foil pans and a cup
from the takeaway dump at a mutt's house.

I heard a hedgehog and a hare at the shining river.
"This is what happened," my mother said.

Mangle

Through a window – a flocked moon;
but within, a warm bed waiting.

In the street below, lidded by fog and smoke,
a man tried to open car doors.

I watched – heart swallowed –

as if I were a child left to sleep
on a back seat,

with no coins in the ashtray
for breakfast at The Pancake House

in the morning.

The man wrestled more doors.
A woman unearthed bottles from a bin.

If only she would see me,
we could help each other.

I waited, Epictetus behind me murmuring:
None of this is yours, except its meaning.

In my dream (your arm my ballast),
I searched an underwater wreck,

retrieved a hammer, tins of beans,
a photo of you with young black hair.

All the while, a child stood ankle-deep
in water.

She played with stones, building a wall,
although it would fall,

threading pebbles through her fingers,
her shins so cold the bones

took shackles
and did not feel them.

On the bank, a washerwoman
rinsed underclothes and shrouds,

fed linen through the mangle,

and we spread it on the grass to air
for next time.

Neighbourhood Rapist

This was dark. He slipped through the sliding glass doors
of the house to the patio. The light in the trailer
parked in the driveway flickered on and off.
He found his ghost jacket and his ghost shoes,
a ghost cap, too. His wife lay on their bed
likes a stone gone cold at the rim of a campfire.
He paused in the lightless driveway
while a street lamp across the river-black road
bled through a break in the sidewalk.
A cat slid through a hole in the dark
to wail at our door; it grew colder.
A shuffle of ghosts, too cold to cry, closed
'round him at the girl's window.
They squeezed the last of light, like flowers
in a press, like the lilies they were, to wake her.
He'd had a rope and a knife for them;
he kept the raped ghost-girls' hopes in a pillbox.
Take one, then take another, as required.

It was earlier than he'd meant but that kind of dark steams
from piles of old boots and locked fridges
when it wants; it crushes frog bones in hibernation,
and eels and snakes in ponds. His breath
was a gas of failure becoming solid.
He pushed the grey spindles of his body
against the girl's window, but it was early enough
that no one dreamed it was nothing to do with them
when she screamed. They came from their houses,
and he ran into the field where he dropped on all fours
and growled, a nightmare forsaken by its prey.

Gargoyle / Mute

Leaves sculpt the foundations,
clouds breast the windowsills.

You will not show your fingernails.

Look at your shoes, without laces,
loose on bare feet – they must hurt

as you run from one granite light into another
and your stone tongue splinters.

Dark Rooms

Brett's owl flies from the rafters,
talons extended.

It is dark up there,
and not enough light

down here to save you.

The windows are flesh wounds
in stone.

It was so long ago,

Brett is cigarette-smoke,
varnish, and kind blue eyes;

he could not paint for years,

but he dances
like Chiron in the taverna.

*

The cat trickles downstairs for a snack,
tapping her claws on each step.

Her name is Athena – the same as Brett's owl!
Perhaps that is what has drawn him near.

He glances in, but goes on past the house
and down the hill to the farms,

then up the rocky trail
to the monastery.

The owl shifts and steadies
in the rafters.

Athena, you roost in the grey woods
of hidden threats,

and can reveal what is dead, alive
or revenant.

We feel your gaze on the back of our necks.

Goddess, hunter by right,
spare us and Athena the cat

who is eating tuna
and cleaning her paws.

Have mercy on us.

*

Fossils and stones settle
on tables and shelves;

a downy, powdery owl vomits bones
and blinks a code.
We rest in a doorway
out of the rain.

I lean against you, my only wish –
to be as we are,

lungs filling and emptying

outside the locker of deserted rooms
while everything unfinished unfolds

and returns.

*

How do you appraise an archive?

I ask my elderly friend about someone she'd loved:
"He'd be another old man I'd have to look after," she says.

Back then, though, she would have done anything.

They packed a leather holdall between them;
hand in hand, they towed it to Left Luggage

where one of them pocketed the key,
and the other one ran for the train.

Equinox / The Vet's Side Door

I place the carrier basket on the table.
The cat knows why she is here.

She stirs and stands, her thin spine arched.

I stroke her head until we reach the death we – helpless –
covet.

At home we dig a grave beneath a cedar.
Indoors, we light a candle, set out fruit and flowers.

Twice, grapes and blossoms roll from plinth to floor,
and then the shrine surrenders.

*

A cold wind at the dock.
I sit in a canvas chair

and wrap my knees in blankets.

A man in a tiger-themed sweatshirt
boasts of a secret place to fish.

An old friend with a wooden leg
stomps along the highway.

(I am used to ghosts – their love of drama.)

My mother brings a blue-lined brown ceramic bowl
of soup and fills the space inside me.

The lure drifts long and wide with tide
and current. The hours I cast suspend.

Frayed Linens of Another Life

"Only the Wasteful Virtues Earn the Sun,"
Yeats wrote on headed notepaper,

referring to his great-grandfather
who leapt over the side of a ship

in the Bay of Biscay
to save a woman's hat.

"His dreams were tattered rags
in vest-pockets of hills,

frayed linens of another life."

*

The ferryman knows his oars,
and I know my place.

By land you forage with dogs;
on water you navigate by echo.

At the right moment,
a hat blown out to sea is a ransom.

You may falter at the height,
the drop to low water,

you may come to the end of childhood –
but Orpheus's head is still singing

on the waves.

They Sailed to Lesbos

There's a school on the hill behind
the village of Assos,

a columned portico, rib-caged
in moonlight,

where Aristotle walked
reciting Sappho.

In good weather you imagine
the shore

you can almost see from there
as Lesbos.

One of Sappho's lovers,
new to the island, sighs

for what is absent.

I put my mouth
to the cup of my hand.

In my sleep I have remembered how

to blow a note as sweet
as vernal equinox. I blow,

and the sea unseals a wreck
(so sharp the longing) to bring her.

*

And they sailed to watch the "dumb and shining
and dead" and infinite,

and found their unaccountable natures
beside them at the rail.

They ploughed the sea and offered gifts of light
to those who waded into the dark

to meet them.

Deep

You must be deep in the earth
to find the water of a dream,

your throat thirsting,

arms stretched for more,
dress wet as you walk dry shod

through the kitchen, the bedroom,

the hallway. The secret of the garden
is that it falls silent at night

and the well kindles. Inside it,

a mother sleeps beside her children,
the water clear enough

to shatter coins of moonlight on their faces.

Call to them! But what if they cry out
and drown?

They breathe like fish,

like the pulse of the spring
that feeds the well. This is nothing

you know how to start or finish.

You walk back and forth,
your hair lank as waterweeds

torn from their roots,

asleep because if you awaken here,
you will die of your love for them.

Dark Questions

In the night I have questions:
when will we enter the fires

of the sun's periodicity; is it time to stir,
maybe walk up a hill to a grove of trees

and make an offering?

Where do questions come from?
A comet dives to the drip line of a city

and cuts a rim of ocean.

The urge for closeness is like starshine,
or a figure climbing from the roots of trees.

We are a quiet herd, busy with food,
blanketed with amazement in the dark,

our fears unpeeled.

A voice I sometimes hear before sleep
calls from a higher place,

"She comes! Phaedra comes!"
But which Phaedra does it mean?

Men whistled and brayed in the theatre of Epidaurus,
when Phaedra, helpless with lust for her stepson,

wept onstage.

Pinus pinea crowded the stone tiers and spat
fat seeds of rage.

Or, is it *my* Phaedra, who fled with her kittens
from the van (my van) driven to Mount Olympus

by an unfaithful lover, while my replacement sweated
in the egg sac of my sleeping bag.

Why do I care? Phaedra stares

from the bole of a pine tree, the sun
like tar as her kittens slash the sheets

of sleepers heavy in their smells.

I keep a trust. Phaedra waits for me
through ruins of time and rock and snow,

my hair as white as her own sleek coat,

boot heels scoring the mountain raw. What is it like
to live this long?

Night answers with midnight clarity,
"It is like this."

Stopping at Tiryns

Heat dragged the earth
with its corpse-net.

There was nowhere to shelter
but in clefts of the walls

of ancient Tiryns.

I poured water over my hands,
and onto the stones

where the Cyclopes had set them.

A few trees
crackled their skins.

*

A satyr came through the pines
and peered through the windscreen.

He led to a hut where a table was set
with two cups and a knife.

The black dug-out pupils of olives
shone from a dish.

The forest god sent the boy I was with
for one more cup, and wine.

When the boy returned in the dusk,
my scarf was torn,

and the red earth drained
in red tufts and red bites.

Oh, walls of Tiryns,

have you not seen a woman
with little water

and no basin,

soaping herself clean
in the night, before?

In the world I am from,
where the woods are close,

I'd wade streams
with body and soul

still mine.

I unbind, I unbind
and return.

The Invisible Life of Feeling

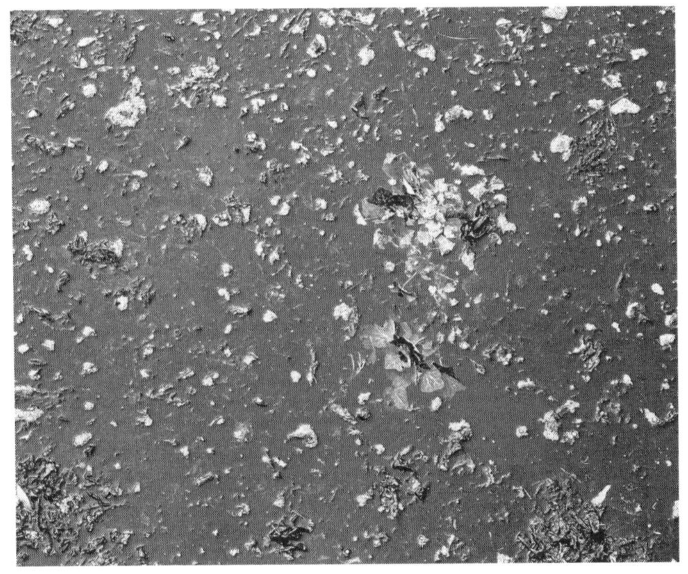

Storm-Lost / Amnesia

Moon on snow, and in its shadow
at the foot of a tree, at the edge of a wood,

at the end of a road stilled in winter –
a tall white hare.

"A jackrabbit," my father says from beside me.
"They came to the woods at night when I was a boy."

We stare at the trees and the moon in the cold
of our memories.

✶

A moment is a drop of ink on the nib of a straight pen
dipped in the well on my desk,

that is, it exists as I need it.

I push a trolley holding a drip bag
attached through a tube and needle into my arm.

My husband removes my earrings.

They say you formed the sky and the seas
and the land and the animals.

I am grateful. I repeat, *grateful.*
Did I already say?

✶

Are you concerned
about gene splicing,

the blurring of animal,
vegetable, and mineral?

Did you imagine all of them
as you?

✶

The teacher calls the roll, and I say, "Present,"
but the desks of my classmates are vacant,

no matter how I try to refill them.

Like the foreign dead, they are
never here where I am.

✶

You do not lie beside me in the night;
you do not guard the door.

You stray through a classroom of empty rows
with your back to the windows.

Listen to birds at the feeder:

they promulgate song,
no matter their quarrels.

*

The words to remember are *cat*, *table*,
and *Paris*.

In a Paris café,
a cat jumped onto the table.

A man orders coffee. Who let him
into this loop of memory?

He broke into my house, pierced his ears
with a sewing needle

and bled onto my manuscripts.

You may cast a shadow
but not hide in it.

*

Implements hang from nails over pencil outlines.

I stroll through houses,
listening to murmurs behind each door.

Someone yawns at a window.
The neighbours turn the lights on

in their kitchens.

*

Fire razes the prairies,
horses stampede the horizon,

grass is orange smoke.

Quail chicks peep from beneath their mother's
blackened feathers.

The mother is like you –

except for the pale bone tracery
of her history.

*

Why am I here?

Did I already ask that question?
Have I asked it before?

*

Hard flooring under the knees,
aunts and uncles, cousins, and grandparents –

a bedtime prayer for all of them,

although what is left of it
will end, perhaps,

with me.

*

Rain falling onto pavement,
rain falling into grass

and upon the afterimages of animals
in the snowy trees.

Gargoyle / Saskatchewan

Snow in the trenches,
no glass in the windows,

the laundry hung outdoors.

She thought of the river,
a neighbour's milk jug,

the warmth of the church bench
on Sundays – where were her shoes? –

and she ran in her slip
and men's broken slippers,

onto the prairie,

the baby snugged under an arm
for delivery.

When she could run no further,
they became these stones.

Cloudy Provinces

I had left the cloudy provinces behind,
I entered the universal, dazzled and desiring.
—Czesław Miłosz

He paused at the grocery exit, plastic bags in hand.
I caught up the steps behind him –

on a shortcut from the nursing home

to buy fruit, flowers, tea,
and cookies for my father.

At the top of the steps, the man fell,
bags ransacked by the wind.

Two doctors drinking coffee,
reached the fallen man ahead of me.

They listened for a heartbeat:
a siren filled the silence.

"Who will carry on my work?" my father says.

When I had purchased fruit, flowers, and the rest,
I steered the shopping cart onto the plaza

to scatter coins and petals.

"I see the kinds of things that I could make,
wooden things," my father says, "but when I awake

they are not there."

Inside my father's room, I read a psalm aloud,

wind reaching from the trees
to stir the curtains.

Slepen

The last time the streets emptied I was twelve years old.
The frozen lanes glistened under lamplight,

each disk a pool of honey gold. At the end of the driveway,
I took off my skate guards, my breath like a circle

of doves. I skated on streets deep-cased in silver,
shadows slicing from my blades.

At the top of the hill, just past the school,

I turned and whirled. Having come this far, I ask,
bones fluorescing still from that long night glide,

"How do birds know to girdle the globe?
Or mate in brief collisions? Make nests of what the wind

blows through the air?" The streets are closed and under
reckoning: I walk the centre line in mask and gloves.

Spirits slip coins onto shuttered eyelids,
and drifting insects *slepen all the nyght*

with open ye.

The Invisible Life of Feeling

for Xan

And there had been the resentment of being strangers in a strange land,
separated from their identities while unable to go back.

—Kapka Kassabova

We were drawn towards birth by birds, they say,
the link between us weightless and invisible,
and learned the world of water from above,
its touch on our skulls as rainfall, and
which hunter-haunted marshes to avoid
and where to land and rest.

We learned the meaning of shadows.

Epictetus says do not ask the athlete how much weight they lift,
but look at the shoulders – the hidden strength
in half-light in the morning when they rise to stretch,
pinion muscle supporting arms, body hair – like feathers.

Light fills my daughter's window – it is summer,
much hallooing from birds when she runs by,
alive together with the earth for this brief time.

As things are, isn't it the height of folly to learn inessential things
when times are so desperately short! – it is Seneca speaking
from his printed land. I glance up from my book
as she re-enters the house, and hear the old stoic ask:
Is this the way to heaven?

A jug on a table is placed to keep our souls, they say:
but one sweep with a hairbrush I found in a dream this morning,
returned my hair to dark, and she and I watched storks
fly to their nests on the rooftops of *Calle Ciudad de Ronda*
at sunset when everyone was young.

On the Bus to the Ferry

I wish I could recall the name of the young man
on a bus, late one night on the way to the ferry.

He said nothing, or little enough,
but in those moments of the ordinary,

the driver shifting gears,
my heart shed leaves

it did not know it had.
I watched his unremarkable face

in the halo of a reading light,
and I let a little of my heart

whisper in the silence.
I hope it did not frighten him.

Once, I hitchhiked three hours north
in the bed of a pickup truck with a boy I'd met,

the gravel road kicking up dust,
the driver slugging from a six pack of Labatt's

between his knees, the sun hot, my mouth a desert
although my life was a tree with fruit and shade.

But now the air is trembling with reminders
of what has withered,

and it turns out there are seasons

in which each spent leaf stem
leaks a little blood and becomes an absence,

the world turning itself inside out
in front of its sons and daughters,

to inspect its sorrowful seams.

Condolences

And in the porches of my ears did pour
The leprous distilment, whose effect
Holds such an enmity with blood of man.
—William Shakespeare

Today, I ask forgiveness for having missed your life.
It was not far as the crow flies, but miles
from my story. I was assailed by a deep lassitude,
as if half-submerged in a lake. I could not decide
between the abyss and one more inhale.
Like the old King of Denmark, I slept beneath a tree,
apples on the boughs above me bagged
and guarded against wasps while a figure
crept through the grass and murmured venom
in my ear. I had thought him well-meaning; he was not.

There was a buzzing, as if a hive were born
within my skull. It established itself. A seeming honey
leaked from my nose and mouth; flies came, and then,
to be brief – I lost my mind. It rolled into a ball,
its crenellations infected, the result of poison
and my unhelpful wonder at what was killing me.
Grief, I thought. But what is grief if not a conversation
with God? Such conversations and delusions I had
(cue the sound of Ages laughing).
I did feel grief. I failed to love those dearest – like you,

my cuz by blood. Apples dropped and rotted; years passed.
I became an orchard, quiet in mind, breathing
with the wind. My brain uncurled and cleared,
its conch shell structures restored as gentle, tuneful
timbrels.

And now I hear that all this time you kept your family safe,
you have ridden bicycles throughout creation!
(I read your posts.) Well done! I am sorry to have missed you,
and I am sorry for your loss. Did your dear one know your talent?
That you assemble the pig ears of the worn-out world,
stitch them into a drum skin on which rain patters?
How as you drum and sing, you hear the sea?

Black Bus on a Winding Mountain Road

after a print by Xu Bing
for dmb

The road is single lane. There are no railings.
Cypresses and pines stipple the cliffs.

White paint above the licence plate is a puff of exhaust,
a rectangle on the back panel is an emergency exit.

The sky is a fish skin of cloud.

Ahead of the bus (or behind it – with Xu Bing
it is hard to tell) a rockfall narrows the way.

A net on the bus rooftop restrains two suitcases,
but no chickens or children, it is not that type

of conveyance.

If a chimney stuck through the roof, it could be your
bus, brakeless, on its way down the hill to the neighbour's.

If the bus were white and plain,
it could be mine on a Yugoslavian mountain road

in the 1970s. A truck sped round the corner:
I reversed until the rear wheels broke the edge.

The track plunged through cloud
to a plain. Women in headscarves

rode donkeys, boys guarded aubergines,
and a girl in a red vest waved.

I had crossed the border from Kosovo to Macedonia
without incident.

In his studio, Xu Bing builds a tiger skin
out of 40,000 filter cigarettes.

His block-print mountains hinge like doors.
His chairs are stone slabs, carved with poetry.

In the Grand Canyon of the Stikine,
goats sew themselves to cliffs above the river.

The river stitches blood and fish and water
to the sea. I remember the roadside shrines

of all those countries.

Cycling

for Kenny Laidlaw

Every day I ride my bicycle: no one around
but shying rabbits and cabbage moths.
Today you rise from the grass beside the path
to catch my eye and ask:
O, how shall summer's honey breath hold out
Against the wreckful siege of battering days?
Why aren't you washing pens and brushes,
the world an egg for tempera, safe with you
until morning?

I ride on and watch the cornflowers bloom against
the faded bricks of warehouses,
and then, a stream goes riddling through a glade.
Few but us will see, when we look up, that wild trees circle higher
than the crows, yet keep their branching feathers;
or that a landscape-worker makes a golden chalice
with her hard hat in the light reflected
from exhausted traffic.

Oh how outwait the siege? Kenny? What do you say?
I hold my breath in case you do not answer,
and all the time there was,
transforms to now without your guidance.

Mariupol Water

In bed at night, I listen to the emptying of Mariupol,
its people slipping on shoes, into cars, along the secret paths
of their bodies. They are the silence inside missiles
and bombs. They are the silence.

I hear gulls on my roof waking in their nests.
A helicopter takes off from the nearest Coast Guard station
to find a fishing boat, or a tug with engine trouble,
or a paddleboarder swept lately out to sea
with the clock of heavens numbering her breaths.

Below black water, submarines snarl through whale pods,
dispersing calves that call and seek their mothers
through deep-water halls, asking *Where? And how?*
And why? Still, there must be people living.
It is best to believe in spring.

Our hearts have seven chambers in a castle within.
St. Teresa says each leads from light to light,
or is one of seven luminaries – the Moon,
Mercury, Venus, the Sun, Mars, Jupiter, or Saturn –
and casts a net of prayer around Earth's
central fires. I listen for rats, but no walls remain
for them to scale.

It is not the Pleiades that rain down fire
on citizens in roofless basements. I count backwards
so I may fall asleep again and dream the helicopter
safely to its mission, the whale calves reunited with their pods,
and no more innocents to die. It is best to believe in spring,
and yet I hear the draining wells and emptying cisterns
of Mariupol.

Dark Driving

for Rachel Wyatt

The boy drove fast
and badly on the road

between forest and cliff.

Dark smeared the car windows
with hands you couldn't quite see

in front of you.

The boy said, "Look at me!"
"I want to get out," I said,

and the boy said,
"Why should I save you?"

Decades passed. Dust and dust.

Night boats stalled
in the sea.

Dog Cerberus flitted
between trees at the shore

as I drove the borders
of the underworld.

Rachel stepped into the road.

Her hand-held lamp once pierced the dark
of the Blitz.

Shadows crossed the highway – harmless,
ahead of us.

"I will take care of you," she said.

"Saving each other
is why we are here."

All souls sank into the foam
as the darkness lightened

and the view through the windscreen
thinned to everyday ruin.

The fishers' freshly wingèd vessels
caught the tide and –

Rachel, was that you
unfurling sunrise?

Dark Love / Fairy Dark

To escape from the dreams of others or to have a private, a secret dream, the Frin must go out alone into the wilderness. And even in the wilderness, their sleeps may be invaded by the strange dream visions of lions, antelope, bears, or mice.

—Ursula Le Guin

Gargoyle / Nest

I let go all threads.

I bit through the knots
wrapped around my fingers.

I set loose all tethered birds.

For months, for years, I lived
to see if they'd return,

which ones sang,

which held their nerve
or hid their nests.

My hands nested, too.

They made a bowl
out of the stone I had become,

and cradled rain.

Life by Water

I was thinking of the poets I have spent time with,
an uncurtained night window in front of me,

a lamp on and somebody sleeping in the next room,
another behind a screen around a bed on the floor above –
a quietness informed by breath. One poet said she lived

next to a river and its life became her thoughts:
they were like water striders easing into a current.
I do not know how cold she was, or if she was hungry.
I did not think of other lives that awaited her.
Poetry was her love of species – especially kinds
of disregarded insects. She refused to kill,
and that became her existence. My brother lures mice
into boxes with trapdoor lids smeared with peanut butter.
He frees them in the meadow, but do they flee
or re-enter the bloodstream of the house?
I have wondered about reincarnation

and the point of words shaped into a song that may never
be sung. We might float down the river next summer
or take the path through the woods,
or descend to the street on stone steps
so steep and worn you must hold to the rail or fall.
A man carries a propane tank

up five floors to my door so I'll be warm enough
to write poetry. I used to dream of someone listening,
mice in the walls, a moth against the spotlit window
as I shared a candle with the poet on the riverbank.
I counted her syllables, I learned her breath
and how to let it go.

A Tale of Love & Enema

A deer walked into a dream.
It lay down on the boulevard.

Meanwhile, the mother was at the sink
in the bathroom, between the boy and girl.

She held up the boy's soiled underwear.
He was sorry! He wouldn't do it again!

She had reached her limit.

She hung a filled red rubber bag
from a hook above the bathtub –

a hose slacked from it.

Wolves with bearded nostrils
pressed muzzles to the windows.

No one answered the door,
but the girl followed the wolves anyway.

In the car, the mother's tears
were seed pearls

trickling from a broken necklace:
they nested within a handkerchief

stored in her suit cuff.
What is love but a sequence of wishes?

The deer observed from a distance.

The doctor wrote scrips for pills,
the deer left the verge with its fawns

and stepped through the split
of the world.

Prayer to St. Moluag / Overdose

This includes miracles such as... Moluag's miraculous transportation across the sea upon a stone. —CAROLYN MCNAMARA

It must be night – the kettle on for camomile tea,
a lighted window across the road, and a woman at the window
facing the sea. Spirits coalesce at her rooftop and above the B&B
next door, and in the smoke of a cruise ship probing the harbour –
over the serial rapist's house, too (but those are phantoms
of broken girls).

The woman has been at the window since her brightness left;
now clouds sieve the moon through the four directions,
not that the houses turn but we have lost our compass.
Ambulances came and went, the paramedics slow-walking
orange kitbags. None of us breathed too deeply not knowing
the boy's name, yet sure of his shape on the gurney.

What matters tonight is what the woman said to her son
before the paramedics closed the body bag, and the last thoughts
of the suicide in the B&B last week. The HAZMAT team and police came
in daylight and later on, the carpet cleaners: but what if I had gone out
to look at the stars, next door's window open nearby;
what if I had cried my astonishment at the beauty in the dark
before he made his choice?

Sometimes, the boy across the street shouted from the upper window
where his mother now sits; or ran down the stairs to stop her
taking the car. Whatever he said, was with the weight of his life.

We could see how hard it was – it was the end of a season,
a threat of flames still in the smoke drift. Three times he walked
from the house to the car in bare feet, clasping pillows and blankets,
the last time with a folded foam mattress locked under his chin
though he didn't go anywhere.

At dawn I sweep the driveway, then kneel in the garden.
"St. Moluag," I whisper to the earth, "we find ourselves
in a shipwreck. They say you help the helpless, why not help us
instead of crossing the sea on a stone to strike an image?
You may defy the rules and not sink and drown,
but we are sea-battered and tired of searching for land."

It has been dry all summer, no rain until today. A cruise ship sounds
five blasts of danger to a fishing boat lolling in slack tide,
its captain a dreamer listening to music while the ship's passengers
are filming from the decks.

"St. Moluag, they say a prayer is never too late.
Leaning against the building stones of your church
set in a field among cows and sheep, we did our best
as visitors, not to disturb the calm. There was a quiver
of kindness at the font, and like a ghost of myself
in a loose bathrobe, out on a day pass that time I was mad,
I believed that at the moment of birth the world comes right,
and God knows that it is good."

St. Moluag / Night School

As they raced across the loch they were nearly neck and neck,
though Columba started to inch out ahead of Moluag. In order
to beat Columba and thus secure dominion over the island,
Moluag cut off his pinky finger and flung it from his boat onto the beach.

—Carolyn McNamara

St. Moluag, you have worked at night
by candlelight, your hands cold, your bones
aching like broken oars. Nobody said, when you were
new, cheeping to the world on thin legs,
slipping in the grass to the shore while the sea
filled your view and drew you,
that creation would drain your breath.

Your hands have lost grip on the curragh,
your eyes cloud for good, and neither knees nor neck
will bend to pray. You were birthed
on a stream of blood and fed at your mother's breast,
you ate porridge, and had a friend to mend you
with a touch.

Now you groan and gather pages on which to write
the tale of the saint you tried to best.
What will you do when the candle burns out
and he is remembered, and you aren't?

Become like that bee near sleep or death,
embalmed with cold on the windowsill,
maybe dream a little honey from the air
and suck imagined sweetness
from its comb.

Finding Voznesensky (but not St. Moluag) in the UBC Library, 1968

Whatever is past is past. So much the better.
But I bite at it as at a mystery.
—Andrei Voznesensky

How do you remain human
in this world? I asked, opening books

of divination. (I would have asked St. Moluag

if I'd known him.) At night I walked my loneliness
through fenced yards of machinery

to a still point beyond the Klieg lights

where I conversed with mice and voles and a cat
that elbowed thin grasses aside.

No one's talent withstands their own long scrutiny.

How stripped of hope I appeared when I found
your words four floors underground

on a grey metal shelf

where fluorescent lighting crazed green cement walls.
Here I discovered pine trees, cedars, and the voices

no one speaks of unless to silence them.

You crossed fields of ice to get to my country,
your forests my forests, their green my green,

the sea as cold. Virgil slipped from tree to tree

behind you. His imploring hands carried the spent world,
while you filled your pockets with seed pods.

I had looked for you without knowing it.

It was like sitting down with friends to dine
in the bomb sites of bare fields, believing

in "something deeper within us / which
we do not understand."

"Nobody escapes the bonfire: /
if you live – you burn,"
you howled

like a woman in a phone booth

calling late at night for someone who never answers.
(I was that woman.) I needed sleep,

but I hiked the trail to the beach instead,

with the dust of my premature burial transformed
by the slow drift of a blessing in my backpack,

to become what it would become.

Shadows

The world is as it always was,
full of shadows and anticipation.
—Adam Zagajewski

In a county of the night
I unpack my suitcase:

no cupboard is forbidden to me,
everyone wishes to talk.

No one says, "Why are you here?
We'd forgotten all about you,"

or worse, "Why did you abandon us?
Why is there no news?"

Those I thought dead are waiting.
Is it my birthday? I want to know,

but dawn is breaking

and my companion is a shadow
that draws a path through snow

before it falls.

I put on its coat, arms into its sleeves,
and walk out of the night,

to find my shoes.

Confession Gothic

Many earths on earth there be
Whom I love mine own shall be.
—Kathleen Raine

In the end, it is only a box in a dream where you lie
with your babe. We do not talk about why you are there,

or how you fought. It was for your own good,
and that of the child. You did not look after her

like he said.

He left a square, covered with net,
over your mouth:

it should have been enough (for breath). He meant you to rest.

I write like any poet who wishes to confess
more than a metaphor.

In New York, Maggie said that a great-aunt
told of a woman in a coffin,

with a bruised face, and a babe in her arms: "The woman was
your great-grandmother," Maggie said.

He was a brute, a drunk who one time pushed Maggie's

relative down the stairs: she was not my kin –
half the children in that house

were fatherless, the mothers in and out of marriages,
out the front door, down the steps

and into the funeral wagon.

In a too bright café, late at night,
Maggie said, "Here are the papers –

birth and marriage certificates, the census,
unexplained deaths at the same address.

These will bring them back to life."

I reopen the story: this time he does not drink,
is never late for supper,

on weekends takes my great-grandmother and the newborn
to the park in afternoon light.

He has money for coffee.

He untangles a strand of her dark hair to kiss.
"Until death," he says and means it this time.

In such fashion, frozen seeds are blown to nest,

and no babe with time spiked to its skull,
sobs behind the backlit café glass.

Path of Totality

for Rachel

There must be a key! someone shouted in my dream,
and shook out the pockets of my raincoat.
Let us be clear: if there was a key, I have lost it.
Is it any wonder I feel guilty? I have no sensible story
to tell, but I am the one who forgot to bring a View-Master disc
from home to school to watch a solar eclipse.
We went outside, the door of the classroom locked –
there was no escape from the day.
Light dropped through trees like shedding fruit,
then a shield like the shutter of a footlight
slid over the sun. Without my lens of muted plastic,
I could not look. Instead, I viewed the flexed knees
of my classmates, and my gaze slipped
to the unmown grass – house-thatch for sparrows, palaces
for insects. I stooped to study a maze-work of scent
while others surveyed the sky through dark transparencies,
and the earth turned the illuminated pages
of its Urtext.

Night Shift

in memory of Lillian and Cora

I cannot sleep, St. Moluag. The woman in the bed next to me
is a friend of my mother's. Her limbs rattle in the darkness
as she weeps. Dear Saint: she has made a ghost of herself
for her husband because there is no kind word in him.
She reads good books – she had hoped to be a scholar
and a poet – but he sends her to the kitchen with his tea three times
when my mother and I visit. It is too hot, too cold, not strong enough.
Where is the demi-cream he likes? He smiles throughout his
"Thank-you-dears," and taps his fingers to her shuffle
in and out with the entablature of her tray.

It was not wrong to take the pills; it was bad luck he came home
at all. I said, "I hope you are feeling better," when we shared the bathroom
sinks. "Hope," she said, her face mud-soft below the smoke and veil
of under eye circles. St. Moluag, they called you "Little Leaping Trickster":
you taught that gifts are a trick of the light when they make seals
swim up to the altar. What's the point? Who asks for it?
And why would they?

*

It is just me, again, St. Moluag.
They say you have a soft spot for the troubled.
The night shift nurse arrives: "Would you like a cup of tea?"
she whispers. I put on my slippers and dressing gown and sit in the dark
to watch the windows of the apartments opposite. In one, a poet
from Fort St. James, sings to his baby. In another, a dentist retrieves
baby ghost teeth which float through the chains of his dreams.

St. Moluag, protect me from a sadness which carves the heart
like a calving iceberg. The night has become a narrow snowstorm
through which I am hurrying to carry water.

*

St. Moluag, I lie awake in the night with the memory
of a woman with cropped blonde hair, a strong woman
of the type my father knew when he harvested
in Manitoba and women wore kerchiefs
and could handle a plough.
She sat in a chair in the hallway and said,
"Go outside and watch the stars,
for they are your youth and sorrow, and are formed
like the bodies of whirring insects."
Sometimes we held hands.
But after the last round of ECT, she gripped my wrist, her torso
wrapped like a caryatid's. Sounds I could not decipher
leaked from her lips. She said "Hell," maybe, or possibly, "Heaven."
A shudder ate her eyes, and she tipped onto the floor of that cureless
corridor. At noon, in the shade of aspens, you may eat bread and apples,
leave your clothes near the roots, and wade in a body with the belly
and breasts of an Artemis, into the world's cold stream. "Have courage,"
she said to me when they took her. (I know she said it.)
What were you looking for, Cora, and for whom? Tell us what happened,
and where are the sons who occupied the farm, brought you here
and felled the trembling aspens of summer?

Buffalo Gaze

Polly was still there, in the house from which a buffalo gazed
at me from an upstairs window. She was tending the garden,
the rhododendron tree – two storeys tall. It took time
to understand who was cutting roses or trimming
the hedge because she changed wigs daily.

She brought squash and cucumber plants across the road to us,
and told a story of seven ghosts of young officers
who transited the stairs to the bedrooms in dress uniforms.
Dancers whirled down the front steps to the garden,
the women gloved to the elbows. (Polly's garden gloves
were wrist-length.) The soldiers drilled on the parade ground
where my neighbours walk their dogs and the serial rapist
crouched when he was cornered.

Drywallers lived in the buffalo suite. They drove trucks into
my driveway to turn around. They waved. I waved. Trebles sat
on the windowsill on Friday nights, laughing to music
until her boyfriend moved in. He steered her up the street
and down to show her black eyes and bruises, her arm in a sling.
Polly said he beat Trebles with a hammer. He sold drugs
from his car. Trebles' bruises healed, but she was a little slow
in speech. She left a potted plant at the end of my driveway
the day she was evicted (the boyfriend in jail). She said she hoped
I would look after it, and I did, and it flowered. I waved goodbye
to the drywallers, too. It took Polly and the manager two weeks
to clear the garage. Polly worried about rats. Then she moved out,
and the house went up for sale. Students leased the main house,
and a mother and son rented the buffalo suite. He carried
their belongings up the stairs.

All summer they took towels and picnic bags to the car,
she in pink and orange summer dresses, he in shorts
and sunglasses. When they fought, he cried from an upstairs
window that he hated his life and her.

I saw the buffalo when I was sleepless:
it was the dark moon opposite, its fur robe a warning
to my species. After the last overdose, the ambulance stayed
for hours, the mother at one window, the buffalo
at the other. Oh buffalo, who called you here as witness?
Candles burn beside you in sunlight, the ghosts too occupied
with memories to pause for another's sadness. But you belong
like the pulse does to the body, like skin and bone to each other,
and the eyes to light over prairie grasslands. I was born there, too,
where the trouble with the dead is that they follow you
like dust in the rearview mirror.

Notes

Epigraph

"God before… be darkened." Alexander Carmichael, "Augury of Mary." *Carmina Gadelica, Hymns and Incantations, in 6 vols* (Scottish Academic Press: 1972), Vol. V, ed. Angus Matheson, 267.

This Was Dark

A suite of poems, primarily from this section, was awarded the Ruth and David Lampe Poetry Prize, 2023 and published in *Exile Magazine* 46.2.
—*Horror / This Is What Happened*: "Some day… long ago." Pär Lagerkvist, *Evening Land,* trans. by W.H. Auden and Leif Sjöberg (Wayne State University Press: Detroit, 1960), 49.
—*Mangle*: Epictetus was a Stoic philosopher c. 50-135 AD.
—*Frayed Linens of Another Life*: John Donohoe of John's Bookshop is cited in an article by Michael Parsons in *The Irish Times*: "I also remember buying at auction a wonderful handwritten quote by William Butler Yeats dated April 27th, 1916. On his headed notepaper was written "Only the Wasteful Virtues Earn the Sun." He is referring to his great grandfather, who jumped over the side of a ship in the Bay of Biscay to save a woman's hat that had blown in the wind. Yeats's mother used to warn her children not to waste their potential like this relative. I wondered, considering the date on the quote, was this his initial view of the 1916 Rising? www.tinyurl.com/DonohoeIT – or scan:
—*They Sailed to Lesbos*: "dumb and shining / and dead." Robert Louis Stevenson, "Songs of Travel, vi," *Collected Poems* (Rupert Hart-Davis: London, 1950), 248.
—*Stopping at Tiryns:* Tiryns was one of the most important centres of Mycenaean Greek culture c. 1400-1200 BC. Its walls, now ruins, were said to have been built by Cyclopes.

The Invisible Life of Feeling

—*Cloudy Provinces*: "I had left… and desiring." Czesław Miłosz, "Bypassing *Rue Descartes*," *New and Collected Poems 1931-2001* (Penguin Modern Classics: London, 2005), 393.

—*Slepen*: "all the nyght with open ye." Geoffrey Chaucer, "General Prologue," *The Canterbury Tales*, line 10.

—*The Invisible Life of Feeling*: "And there… unable to go back." Kapka Kassabova, *To the Lake* (Granta: London, 2020), 328; "Epictetus… feathers." Adapted from Epictetus, *Discourses*, trans. by Robin Hard (Oxford World Classics: Oxford, 2014); "As things are… desperately short." Seneca, *Letters from a Stoic* (Penguin Classics: London, 2014); *Calle Ciudad de Ronda* is a street in Seville, Spain where I lived.

—*Condolences*: "And in the porches… blood of man." (Shakespeare, *Hamlet* 1.5.63-64).

—*Black Bus on a Winding Mountain Road*: Xu Bing is a Chinese artist b. 1955.

—*Cycling*: "O, how… of battering days." (Shakespeare, *Sonnet* 65.5-6).

—*Dark Driving*: The witty and beloved playwright, novelist and short-story writer, Rachel Wyatt, died July 7th, 2024. She haunted coffee shops and could have been a spy like her father. Instead, she was that rare friend who was both wise and kind. Cerberus was said by the ancient Greeks to be the watchdog of the underworld.

Dark Love / Fairy Dark

Epigraph: "To escape… for mice." Ursula Le Guin, "Social Dreaming of the Frin," *Changing Planes* (Harcourt: USA, 2003).

—*Life by Water*: The title of the poem is a reference to Lorine Niedecker, *My Life by Water – Collected Poems 1936-1968* (Fulcrum Press: London, 1970).

—*Prayer to St. Moluag / Overdose*: "This includes… upon a stone." Carolyn McNamara, "Feast Day of Moluag," St. Moluag's Coracle (Scotland:

June 25, 2022), www.tinyurl.com/McNamaraSMO – or scan: 

I first came across St. Moluag, the sixth-century Celtic saint, in the bare and beautiful twelfth-century Teampull Mholuaidh, named after him, on the Isle of Lewis. The church was likely built on much older foundations. He was a friend (or rival) of St. Columba, who is more widely remembered; but the name Moluag incorporates the attachment "My Dear" to his birth name and shows the affection in which he was held, especially by those in need of mental healing.

—*St. Moluag / Night School*: "As they raced… onto the beach." *Ibid.*

—*Finding Voznesensky (but not St. Moluag) in the UBC Library 1978*: "Whatever is… a mystery." Andrei Voznesensky, "Nostalgia for the Present" (trans. Vera Dunham and H.W. Tjalsma), 4; and "something deeper… not understand." "Snowdrops" (trans. William Jay Smith and Nicholas Fersen), 81; both in Andrei Voznesensky, *Nostalgia for the Present*, Vera Dunham, and Max Hayward, eds (Oxford: Oxford University Press, 1968). "Nobody… you burn." Andrei Voznesensky, "Fire in the Architectural Institute" (trans. Stanley Kunitz), *Antiworlds*, Patricia Blake and Max Hayward, eds (Oxford: Oxford University Press, 1967), 58.

I have written in the Notes section of *What Is Long Past Occurs in Full Light* (Mother Tongue: Salt Spring Island, 2019) of the importance to me of Voznesensky's work.

—*Shadows*: "The world… anticipation." Adam Zagajewski, "Three Angels," *Without End – New and Selected Poems* (Farrar, Straus and Giroux: New York, 2003), 266.

—*Confession Gothic*: "Many earths… shall be." Kathleen Raine, *The Year One* (Farrar, Straus and Young: New York, 1952), 14-16.

Acknowledgements

Some of these poems were published in the online blogspot *Dusie*, and in print with *Exile Magazine, Grain Magazine, The Malahat Review, The New Quarterly*, and *The Scottish Review*. "Storm Lost / Amnesia" appeared in *The Hippocrates Book of the Brain*, 2022; "Mariupol Water" was published in *Poems in Response to Peril*, 2022.

My gratitude to Isabel Huggan, Rhonda Lillard, Susan Musgrave and the late Rachel Wyatt for their advice and encouragement; to Seán Virgo for his perceptive and patient editing; to Xan Shian for her evocative photographs; and to Michael Elcock whose love and support made the writing possible.

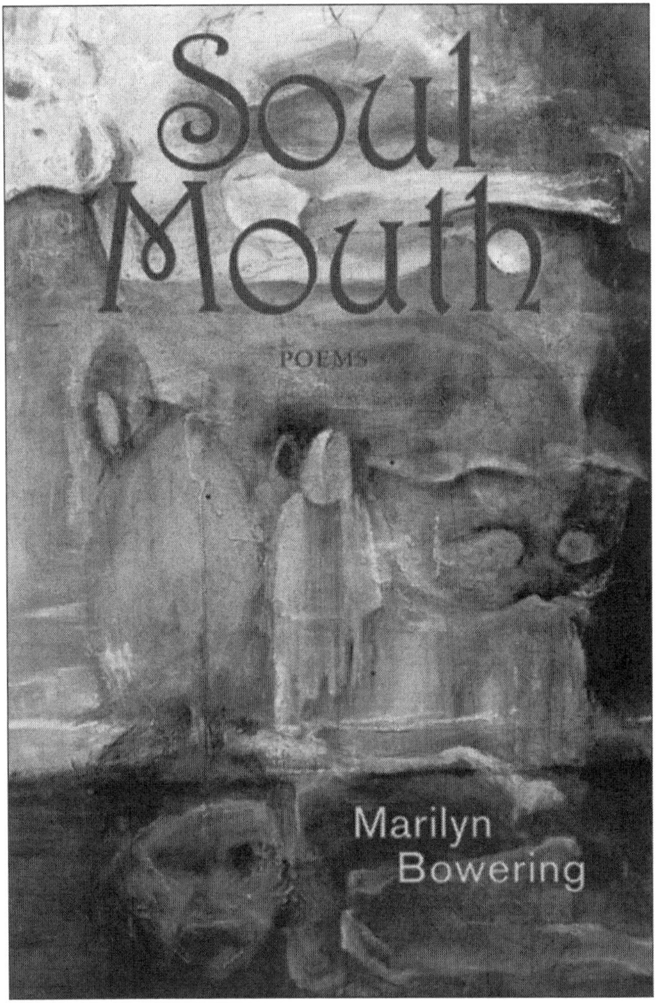